Kaputnik

A Comedy in One Act

by

Frank Semerano

NEW YORK HOLLYWOOD LONDON TORONTO

SAMUELFRENCH.COM

Copyright © 2008 by Frank Semerano
ALL RIGHTS RESERVED

CAUTION: Professionals and amateurs are hereby warned that *KAPUTNIK* is subject to a royalty. It is fully protected under the copyright laws of the United States of America, the British Commonwealth, including Canada, and all other countries of the Copyright Union. All rights, including professional, amateur, motion picture, recitation, lecturing, public reading, radio broadcasting, television and the rights of translation into foreign languages are strictly reserved. In its present form the play is dedicated to the reading public only.

The amateur live stage performance rights to *KAPUTNIK* are controlled exclusively by Samuel French, Inc., and royalty arrangements and licenses must be secured well in advance of presentation. PLEASE NOTE that amateur royalty fees are set upon application in accordance with your producing circumstances. When applying for a royalty quotation and license please give us the number of performances intended, dates of production, your seating capacity and admission fee. Royalties are payable one week before the opening performance of the play to Samuel French, Inc., at 45 W. 25th Street, New York, NY 10010.

Royalty of the required amount must be paid whether the play is presented for charity or gain and whether or not admission is charged.

Stock royalty quoted upon application to Samuel French, Inc.

For all other rights than those stipulated above, apply to: Samuel French, Inc., at 45 W. 25th Street, New York, NY 10010.

Particular emphasis is laid on the question of amateur or professional readings, permission and terms for which must be secured in writing from Samuel French, Inc.

Copying from this book in whole or in part is strictly forbidden by law, and the right of performance is not transferable.

Whenever the play is produced the following notice must appear on all programs, printing and advertising for the play: "Produced by special arrangement with Samuel French, Inc."

Due authorship credit must be given on all programs, printing and advertising for the play.

ISBN 978-0-573-66293-5   Printed in U.S.A.   #16329

No one shall commit or authorize any act or omission by which the copyright of, or the right to copyright, this play may be impaired.

No one shall make any changes in this play for the purpose of production.

Publication of this play does not imply availability for performance. Both amateurs and professionals considering a production are strongly advised in their own interests to apply to Samuel French, Inc., for written permission before starting rehearsals, advertising, or booking a theatre.

No part of this book may be reproduced, stored in a retrieval system, or transmitted in any form, by any means, now known or yet to be invented, including mechanical, electronic, photocopying, recording, videotaping, or otherwise, without the prior written permission of the publisher.

IMPORTANT BILLING AND CREDIT REQUIREMENTS

All producers of *KAPUTNIK* must give credit to the Author of the Play in all programs distributed in connection with performances of the Play, and in all instances in which the title of the Play appears for the purposes of advertising, publicizing or otherwise exploiting the Play and/or a production. The name of the Author *must* appear on a separate line on which no other name appears, immediately following the title and *must* appear in size of type not less than fifty percent of the size of the title type.

KAPTUNIK was first presented by the Lost Hollywood Players at the Grove Center Theater in Burbank, California on November 16, 2007. The play was produced by Victoria Watson and Adam Winkler; directed by Curtis Krick; Special Script Contributions by Tiffany Plunkett; set design by Max Glen; set construction by Alex Wallmark; stage managed by Kim O'Bannon; assistant stage manager Kyle Giddens. The cast was as follows:

MYLES	Fleet Cooper
BLAINE	Christopher B. Smith
MRS. VOSKOVEC	Deidre Moore
RIMSKY	Adrian Colon
TATIANNA	Patricia Rigney
HALI	Victoria Watson
ANNOUNCER	Richard Heft

CHARACTERS

MYLES STANTON: Chief Astronomer and Administrator of the Drywood Observatory
BLAINE: His Assistant
HALI: A Frequent Visitor to the Observatory
MRS. VOSKOVEC: A Mysterious Woman
RIMSKY: Subordinate to Mrs. Voskovec
TATIANNA: Another Subordinate to Mrs. Voskovec

SCENE

The Drywood Observatory on a high plateau somewhere in the New Mexico Desert.

TIME

October 7th, 1957 in the hours following Sputnik's launch.

For Ione Semerano, Mary Jane Semerano and Gioconda Giraldi

Scene I

(SETTING: *The working area of an observatory, circular in layout indicating the dome the telescope is housed in. However, to reach the eyepiece of the telescope and the camera, a portable four-step stairway with a landing on top must be climbed. There is a window in the back framing a view of the desert showing a cactus in the background and the night sky beyond. The background behind the window will change periodically and very slowly accompanied by a low rumbling sound, simulating the rotation of the dome. There are three doors: One leading to the outside, another to a bathroom and a third to a storage area below. Other features include a control station, photographic equipment, desk, small icebox and cot. A solitary picture adorns the walls of the dome; a large photograph of the observatory taken at night.)*

(AT RISE: *Lights come up to an empty stage.)*

(A voice with static in the background is heard over the radio.)

ANNOUNCER. "Living among us and determined on our ultimate destruction are the secret agents of the enemy."

(Three individuals in trench coats, a **MAN** *and two* **WOMEN***, rise from the seats in the front row and walk onto the stage. They are wearing Fedoras, sunglasses and carrying cameras.)*

ANNOUNCER. *(cont'd)* "They walk and work beside us without our once being aware of who they really are or of their objective."

(The indviduals photograph everything in the observatory.)

ANNOUNCER. *(cont'd)* "They are skilled in the art of deception. Rarely if ever do these foreign vermin fit the suspicious Hollywood stereotype of spies in trench coats, fedoras and dark sunglasses."

(The three individuals quickly stop taking pictures and look at themselves and each other and appear slightly embarrassed.)

ANNOUNCER. *(cont'd)* "Patriots, you must be vigilant. Be aware. Be suspicious. How great the shame of those misguided Americans who fall prey to these enemy agents and become their willing tools."

*(One of the individuals turns off the radio. **MYLES**, dressed in a lab coat, rushes rushing down the aisle in the audience and confronts the three individuals on stage.)*

MYLES. Please put that down, this isn't a souvenir shop. You can't buy that. We can't get started until you take your seats.

*(The individual tries to put some money into **MYLES** hands, who refuses it. A small object **MYLES** and he are fighting over drops to the ground and breaks. **MYLES** grabs the money and after some effort herds the reluctant three back into their seats in the audience.)*

MYLES. *(To audience)* Sorry to keep you waiting. I'm always so happy to welcome tour groups to our important facility. You know, I actually became an astronomer by accident. I took my brother's place on a science class field trip to the observatory when he was too sick to go. I guess you could say when I looked at Mars, Jupiter and Saturn for the first time I didn't planet. Ha, ha, ha...

(The three individuals in trench coats get up and walk out, crossing the stage and exiting through the rear door of the observatory.)

MYLES. No refunds!

(**BLAINE** *storms in through the front door of the observatory covered in feathers, his face cut and bruised. He puts on some iodine.*)

MYLES. Ah, my devoted assistant Blaine! Finally back from cleaning that hawk's nest off the telescope, eh? Ready to take over the next tour?

(**BLAINE** *coldly turns towards* **MYLES** *about to say something but stops, shifts his shoulders around as if to scratch an itch, and pulls out an egg from behind his collar. He quietly puts it down and starts to put a Band-Aid over his cheek.*)

(*The phone rings.* **BLAINE** *just looks at* **MYLES**.)

MYLES. Blaine, the phone's ringing.

(**BLAINE** *spits out a feather.*)

MYLES. Tell you what, why don't I get it? You rest your voice. (*To audience*) Excuse me.

(**MYLES** *picks up the phone.*)

Hello, Drywood Observatory. Ah, Fredericks! How's everything over at Palomar? What? You received my assistant's application for a job? And my outstanding letter of recommendation? Let me call you back.

(**BLAINE** *starts to walk away, but* **MYLES** *grabs him by the collar*)

BLAINE. Wrong number, sir?

MYLES. I feel violated. Why didn't you tell me? We always got along, I thought, like birds of a...

(*Blaine opens his mouth to protest and coughs feathers into* **MYLES**' *face.*)

MYLES. Perhaps not the best turn of phrase. Blaine, why don't you tell me the problem?

BLAINE. Sir, when I first accepted this assignment you assured me quarters would be available.

MYLES. And they still are. Four for a dollar.

BLAINE. And when you said you'd give me one of the

highest salaries in the state, I assumed you meant the amount of money in the check, not the elevation where it was paid.

MYLES. I see.

BLAINE. And when you said there would be an opportunity to rise quickly I didn't know it would be because I'd be working on top of an active volcano.

MYLES. Blaine, splitting hairs is for barbers. Oh…I can I convince you to stay when I'm can't convince myself.

(**MYLES** *leans against the telescope.*)

BLAINE. I don't understand sir.

MYLES. Look at me, Blaine. You're young. But me? I'm like that telescope. This observatory is obsolete. Nobody wants to use a 32" telescope. Not when Mt. Palomar has a 200" telescope.

BLAINE. I thought it's not the size of your telescope but how you use it that counts.

MYLES. I tell myself that every day. Blaine, has anyone ever complained that you weren't able to penetrate far enough into the dark void? That your explorations left them cold and unexcited?

BLAINE. I don't know how to answer that, sir. But fine, if you say so, you are just like this telescope. *Exactly* like this telescope. A mighty tool for discovery!

(**BLAINE** *goes over to the control station and presses a button. Nothing happens.* **MYLES** *walks over to the wall and kicks it and the dome starts rotating.*)

(*After a moment there is a terrible grinding noise and everything stops.*)

BLAINE. Useless. Not worth carting down the hill for scrap metal! We might as well just dig a hole right here and bury the piece of junk, nobody will miss it!

(**MYLES** *quietly sits down and puts his face in his hands.*)

BLAINE. Sir, I didn't mean to say you were *exactly* like this telescope.

(MYLES moves over to the window and just looks out wistfully.)

BLAINE. *(Without enthusiasm)* Dr. Stanton…I want you to know I'll work here with you just as long as you'd have me.

MYLES. Really? You promise?

BLAINE. Just don't remind me there are bigger lenses on my glasses than on this telescope.

MYLES. It's a deal! Now let's get on that gearbox.

(MYLES turns on the radio and both BLAINE and MYLES work on the gearbox of the telescope to the beat of the music. The music suddenly stops.)

ANNOUNCER. We interrupt this program to bring you the following special news bulletin. The next sound you hear will be a signal transmitted by the Soviet Union's spacecraft, Sputnik, the world's first artificial satellite. From the day forward, the old shall forever be separated from the new.

(Static is heard and then, slowly rising in volume, the "beeping" of the satellite as it passes overhead. BLAINE and MYLES stop what they are doing.)

MYLES. The sound of the human race stirring in its cradle.

BLAINE. A signal to other worlds. Here we are! Come and get us!

MYLES. Martians again. Blaine, hasn't it ever struck you that the recent flurry of UFO sightings started at the time the Russians got the nuclear bomb? It's just paranoia.

(BLAINE grabs a handful of papers and places them in MYLES hands.)

BLAINE. These spectrographic analyses don't lie.

MYLES. Look at that atmosphere. It's a photochemical soup. No one could live on Mars.

BLAINE. That's a spectrograph of Los Angeles. This one is Mars.

MYLES. Yes, yes, and looking at it I reach the same conclusion. The small amount of oxygen in the atmosphere would force any life forms to evolve very large lungs. Imagine a race of beings walking around with artificially large chests. Say, am I looking at data from Los Angeles again?

BLAINE. With Sputnik in orbit one day they'll have observatories in space proving what I say.

MYLES. Observatories in space? Making this place even more obsolete?

(MYLES throws down the wrench.)

MYLES. The end of our journey. It's been quite an odyssey. I remember as a boy I would run over to my friend's house to use his telescope... until one night I accidentally broke the telescope. I cried that night. Wept. My stars were gone. And so was that view of the girls' dormitory bathroom.

(BLAINE puts his arm around MYLES.)

BLAINE. I'm sorry Myles.

MYLES. You know, it's funny. After all we've been through together this is the first time you've called me by my first name.

BLAINE. I know.

MYLES. *Don't* do it again.

(BLAINE removes his arm from around MYLES.)

MYLES. When I no longer had a telescope to use I'd study the constellations. That was my favorite. Virgo – The Virgin. See how the star Arcturus is at her knee and the star Spica helps to form her delicate hand. A classical beauty. Right down to those three minor stars forming the nipples of her breasts. Three nipples? Blaine, how many times have I told you not to draw on the photos!

BLAINE. It wasn't me, sir. Can I look, sir?

MYLES. How old are you?

BLAINE. Old enough.

MYLES. Ever been married?

BLAINE. Not yet.

MYLES. Then no, you can't look. But you are right about one thing. Nobody's been drawing on this photo. It looks like an actual star. A big one. A star where there's not supposed to be one. Get me the star charts.

(BLAINE goes into a filing cabinet. While MYLES waits impatiently, BLAINE removes a shirt, razor, ties, catcher's mitt, and finally retrieves a book.)

BLAINE. Maybe Virgo-The Virgin, has always had three stars...there.

MYLES. I hardly think the ancient Greeks would give the name the Virgin to a wanton hussy with three nipples.

BLAINE. You're right, sir. According to this star chart there is no known star in that position. Are you sure I can't take just a peek?

MYLES. If I can be blunt, Blaine, your problem is you've been living alone too long.

BLAINE. Without living quarters it's been a little hard to meet single women, sir.

(MYLES takes the charts from BLAINE.)

MYLES. You get along well enough with my wife. You should try harder.

BLAINE. With your wife, sir?

MYLES. *(Looking at chart)* Hmmm...Last year nothing was there. So it might be a new star. A major discovery. The world would have to take notice.

MYLES & BLAINE *(Together)* At last, a ticket out of this rat hole!

BLAINE. Too bad Virgo is a summer constellation and we won't be able to see it again until next year.

MYLES. Then I think the first thing we should do is try to find a photo of the same area taken at a later date and see if that object is still there.

(**MYLES** *plows through a filing cabinet and becomes irritated as he removes a series of* **BLAINE***'s personal items from the drawer.* **MYLES** *removes a large folder full of photos and pulls out one out.*)

MYLES. Ah, Here we go. A view taken of the area one week later.

(*He views the photo with a magnifying glass.*)

MYLES. This is restricted airspace. If there were an aircraft flying that night, the local base would have a record of it.

BLAINE. What if the base it came from…wasn't local?

MYLES. Blaine, you've got Martians on the brain! Call the base and ask about anything flying that night. But don't tell them what we're up to. I don't want them thinking I don't know what I'm doing.

(**MYLES** *sits down on the desk on top of the owl's egg.* **BLAINE** *goes to the telephone and* **MYLES** *cleans off his pants and continues examining the plate*)

BLAINE. They'll call us back.

MYLES. Fine, fine.

(**BLAINE** *quietly takes the magnifying glass and walks over to the photo hanging on the wall and begins examining it.* **MYLES** *looks up and sees him.*)

MYLES. Blaine!

BLAINE. I'm just looking. And this is incredible. Not only does Virgo appear to have three nipples but now Cassiopeia seems to have three buttocks.

MYLES. Come over here Blaine. You're a lonely man, aren't you? I think I can help. I know you think of me as a brilliant, virile astronomer whose work has exposed you to the wonders of the universe. But I've been known to bring other things together too.

(**MYLES** *takes a picture out of his wallet and shows it to* **BLAINE**.)

MYLES. What do you think?

BLAINE. That's a very good looking wall sir.

MYLES. That's my niece!

(**MYLES** *takes more pictures from wallet.*)

MYLES. Here, let me put it together with this picture on the right and this one on the left. Oh, and here are the feet.

BLAINE. It...It is a person!

MYLES. I know it's not a great picture but you have to understand I was standing back kind of far.

BLAINE. Why? Was she hungry?

MYLES. Look, Blaine, I haven't seen you with a lot of women.

BLAINE. And if I were standing next to her you still wouldn't be able to see me. Or the rest of the horizon.

MYLES. I'll have you know she's broken a lot of hearts.

BLAINE. Well you can solve that little problem by telling her to stop sitting on her dates.

MYLES. If you don't want to go out with her, just say so!

BLAINE. I don't want to go out with her.

MYLES. Then here. You can take your magnifying glass back. I hope the two of you will be very happy together!

(*The phone rings and* **BLAINE** *picks it up.*)

BLAINE. Drywood Observatory. Oh hello, Major. What's that? No records of anything flying that night. Thank you.

MYLES. Then what was it?

BLAINE. And where is it now?

(*A bright white beam shoots through the window, accompanied by a loud sound increasing in volume. They both cautiously walk out the door.*)

BLAINE. *(O.S.)* Martians!

MYLES. *(O.S.)* MARTIANS!?

(*There is loud commotion, a crash, and a terrible scream. Lights: BLACKOUT.*)

End of Scene I

Scene II

*(**AT RISE:** Lights normal on the floor of the observatory.* **BLAINE** *is sitting in a chair with an ice pack over his eyes, slowly shaking his head.* **MYLES** *looks very apologetic.)*

MYLES. I'm sorry I hit you, Blaine, but you surprised me. You've got to stop yelling, "Martians!" every time someone pulls into the driveway.

BLAINE. The fact you're scared means you believe in Martians too!

MYLES. The *only* thing I admit is that we need more information. I want you to go into the basement and bring up the filters.

BLAINE. But there's a family of wild bobcats living in the basement!

MYLES. And why else would I buy you a box of catnip?

*(**MYLES** hands **BLAINE** a box of catnip.)*

MYLES. Make friends but don't make a mess.

BLAINE. But, but...

MYLES. Get going. Whoever pulled up is probably part of the next tour group and before they show up we have mysteries of science to solve.

*(**MYLES** pushes **BLAINE** through the basement door. There's a roar of angry bobcats. **MYLES** shuts the door, cutting off the sound abruptly. He picks up a wrench and starts working on the telescope's gear box again, crawling underneath. A **WOMAN** walks in through the front door and walks up to him.)*

MYLES. That was quick. Hand me the socket wrench. I wish you'd change your mind about my niece. She's very easy to get along with. Who isn't really. Take Hali for instance. Sometimes she can drone on and on, but I just nod my head and smile. You know why? Because in my mind I am sailing. You know the name of my sailboat Blaine? I call it Freedom. Sometimes when

I'm on Freedom I see a dinghy full of dirty dishes and glasses. Oh they're actually clean because I washed them myself, but Hali says they're still dirty. So I take Freedom and ram that dinghy until it sinks. "That clean enough for you," I ask?

HALI. Not if you're still not using soap.

MYLES. *(Pause)* Blaine, have you been inhaling the helium again?

(**MYLES** *comes up from under the gear box.*)

MYLES. Pussycat. I can explain…

HALI. Don't let it worry you, Myles. Did you forget already? Today's the day.

MYLES. What d- oh! You're right. It's just that with everything that's happened…Did you hear about Sputnik?

HALI. I don't want to hear about Sputnik. You made me a promise two weeks ago and I'm going to hold you to it, mister. I'm all packed.

MYLES. You're sure your parents approve?

HALI. They've been waiting for this day for years.

MYLES. All right then, darling. As of midnight tonight we'll be officially…divorced.

HALI. SO let's go and get it started.

MYLES. What's the hurry about a divorce anyway? It's not like your mother booked a hall for the event and sent out invitations.

(**HALI** *shows him a card.*)

MYLES. Oh. They serve good food there. How come for our wedding she could only afford an oven timer?

HALI. Shall we get going.

MYLES. But I love you. You're the only one I have to care for.

(**BLAINE** *enters quickly through the basement door, his coat shred to pieces, the sound of angry bobcats behind him.*)

BLAINE. *(Gasping)* Antiseptic…Iodine…Bandages Rabies

shots!

HALI. What's going on?

MYLES. Ah-hah! The filters! Told you the catnip would work.

(**MYLES** *grabs the filters.* **HALI** *rushes over to* **BLAINE**.)

HALI. Catnip? What's going on here?

MYLES. What I've been trying to tell you, pussycat. Blaine and I are on the verge of a very important discovery.

HALI. Not tonight you're not. Even during our honeymoon you were...

(**MYLES** *places his hands over* **BLAINE**'s *ears.*)

MYLES. Darling please! Not in front of Blaine. He worships me.

(*He removes his hands from* **BLAINE**'s *ears.*)

MYLES. Blaine, take these tools and go outside and reattach the wires to the dome lights. There's a good lad.

BLAINE. *(Looks out the window)* Out there...? At five o'clock today Mars was only 244,938,476 miles from Earth.

HALI. He's kidding.

MYLES. No. No. No, he's not.

BLAINE. Close enough to almost feel an icy alien hand reaching out.

(**HALI** *gently puts her hand on* **BLAINE**'s *shoulder and He screams.*)

MYLES. Will you settle down. You and your Martians. Now out!

(**BLAINE** *cautiously takes the tools and goes outside and stands on the window ledge and begins working on an electrical box.*)

HALI. Let's go, Myles.

MYLES. I just don't think you've thought out all the consequences.

HALI. We've gone over everything. Let's get in the car, drive across the border and get it over with.

MYLES. What about Toby? Have you thought what it might do to Toby?

HALI. Toby is a hamster.

MYLES. He's bonded to us.

HALI. He's bonded to everything since your glue experiment.

MYLES. My anti-gravitational experiments!

(He picks up a small hamster cage off the desk and tries to shake loose the hamster which is stuck to one side.)

MYLES. Didn't you hear about Sputnik?

HALI. What's that got to do with you?

MYLES. I'm a scientist. Trying to open the windows to the Universe. Would you have me shut them instead like this?

*(He dramatically slams the shutter closed, pushing **BLAINE** off the ledge and sending him falling down. The sound of his body tumbling down the hill makes **MYLES** wince every time **BLAINE** hits something. After a few moments silence.)*

MYLES. What a break! The cactus broke his fall.

*(**HALI** runs over to the window.)*

HALI. Is he ok?

MYLES. His legs are fine. His arms appear ok.

HALI. And he has movement in at least one of his fingers.

MYLES. I SAW THAT, BLAINE!

HALI. I don't want to hear another word. I'm going to powder my nose and then we're going to leave.

(She opens up her luggage and takes out some toiletries.)

MYLES. What about our property?

HALI. Twin cemetery plots is not property.

MYLES. They're very expensive. Those plots put me in a hole.

HALI. You can have them both.

MYLES. That's the thanks I get for trying to provide for the future.

HALI. Myles There are two things I don't look forward to filling up. My gas tank and my cemetery plot.

MYLES. But...

HALI. Maybe if you had spent more time thinking about the present...never mind, it's too late.

(**HALI** *goes into the bathroom as* **BLAINE** *walks in through the front door with several pieces of cactus sticking on him.*)

MYLES. My wife is certainly in a hurry to leave.

BLAINE. Go, Sir. Please.

(**BLAINE** *pulls a piece of cactus off his shoulder.*)

MYLES. She wouldn't leave me if that light turns out to be a great discovery. I wonder what she's got packed in the suitcase?

(**MYLES** *opens it up and pulls out a very sexy and flimsy negligee.* **MYLES** *jaw drops in disbelief.* **BLAINE** *notices.*)

BLAINE. We're in the desert. It's very hot out here.

(**MYLES** *removes an even flimsier negligee.*)

BLAINE. Very, very hot.

(**MYLES** *removes a still flimsier negligee, basically made up of strings.*)

BLAINE. I could use a glass of water right now myself.

(**MYLES** *removes a pair of handcuffs.*)

MYLES. Another man!

BLAINE. At least it's a policeman.

MYLES. Blaine, just what is it you do with your evenings?

BLAINE. I spend them with you.

MYLES. Right. I guess I can't really blame her for leaving me for someone else. I wonder what he's like.

BLAINE. My guess is someone tall, ruggedly handsome, attentive, and fun to be with.

MYLES. I appreciate that, Blaine, but if those things didn't satisfy her the first time around, what makes you think she'll ever be satisfied?

BLAINE. My point was actually…

(**HALI** *exits from the bathroom.*)

HALI. Well, are you ready?

MYLES. Umm…I need to pick up a few of my things yet. They're down at the generator station. I'll get them.

HALI. And get four flat tires while you're at it. Myles, I know you. I'll get your things. And I'll be right back.

(She exits.)

BLAINE. Nice try sir.

MYLES. Blaine, you fool, she's doing exactly what I expected! I need time. I must find the answer to that light before anybody else. It could mean everything. Maybe even my marriage. Now, she doesn't know about the utility tunnel between the observatory and the generator station. We slide down there ahead of her and lock the door.

BLAINE. We?

MYLES. We, me, you. What's the difference?

BLAINE. But don't high voltage wires run through there?

MYLES. Forewarned is forearmed. Now, off you go.

*(He pushes **BLAINE** out the front door. After a moment there is the sound of a scream and electrical discharges as the lights flicker. **MYLES** walks over to the window with a pair of binoculars and looks out at the same time an individual with a camera pops up outside the window and looks in. Neither can see the other until they pan into each other's view simultaneously)*

MYLES & MRS. VOSKOVEC. *(Together)* Whoa! What the…

MRS. VOSKOVEC. *(With a thick Eastern European accent)* No need to being worried. Am average American citizen like yourself. Thanking you now for any courtesies extended to one in need who is having been born in this country just like you.

MYLES. Uh…your car break down?

MRS. VOSKOVEC. Grasp of situation testimony to superiority of American education system, is it not, as practiced under our country's great 34th President, Dwight Eisenhower, for whom I cast many ballots.

MYLES. Many ballots?

MRS. VOSKOVEC. *(Looks in a book)* Er, one ballot. Was humorous political joke, was it not? Permit me to be introducing myself. Am Mrs. Voskovec. Now I coming inside.

(She enters through the front door.)

MYLES. Are you here for the tour group? Alone?

MRS. VOSKOVEC. No. Am average American traveling with average of 2.5 children. Rimsky, Tatianna. Pleased to be entering now.

*(**RIMSKY** and **TATIANNA** enter. They are the same height as **MRS. VOSKOVEC** and both are obviously the same age as she. Although Tatianna tries to pass for a younger child by wearing bows in her hair, and **RIMSKY** attempts the same subterfuge wearing a Daniel Boone Coonskin hat and carrying cotton candy. Working against their disguises is the fact that all three of them are wearing trench coats.)*

MYLES. My, big for their age.

MRS. VOSKOVEC. Is it not so?

(They begin taking pictures of everything.)

MYLES. I'm uh…not really sure I can help you. Perhaps I'd better call a service.

*(**MYLES** runs to the phone but **MRS. VOSKOVEC** blocks his path.)*

MRS. VOSKOVEC. Army or Air Force to be notified for what reason?

MYLES. I meant a tow truck service.

*(**RIMSKY** rips the phone out of the wall.)*

RIMSKY. Sorry to be breaking phone in most unfortunate accident.

MYLES. My phone!

MRS. VOSKOVEC. Not to be worrying at all. Several gold coins for repair graciously offered.

(**TATIANNA** *hands him some gold coins.*)

MYLES. This looks like real gold!

TATIANNA. Can substitute for currencies from any NATO country or Allied Power if more to liking.

MYLES. No. Gold's fine.

MRS. VOSKOVEC. Any other method for communicating with outside world?

MYLES. Well, there is the ham set...

(**RIMSKY** *makes the ham radio fall.*)

RIMSKY. Oh no, bringing now more shame to myself and family for inexcusable clumsiness.

MRS. VOSKOVEC. (*Walking up to broken radio*) Ah Rimsky! For this you will surely not receive the Order of the Vigilant Guardian of the Motherland...

(*She shakes his hand.*)

But instead shall receive severe punishment.

(*She grabs him by the ear.*)

I do not know what to say except please have more gold.

TATIANNA. (*Hands out more gold to* **MYLES**) More gold.

MYLES. Say, I got a transistor radio in my jacket.

MRS. VOSKOVEC. Useful for transmitting movement of suspicious characters?

MYLES. No.

TATIANNA. No more gold.

MRS. VOSKOVEC. Must now administer punishment to errant son, Rimsky. Need small room and ten foot steel rod.

MYLES. Now I don't think that's...

MRS. VOSKOVEC. Please no interference.

MYLES. Well you can use the bathroom over there but as far as a steel rod…

(**RIMSKY** *breaks a support rod off the dome.*)

RIMSKY. Am finding one now! Excellent! Most excellent!

(**RIMSKY** *and* **MRS. VOSKOVEC** *draw together. They look at the other with an intense, passionate longing then just as quickly draw a deep breath and compose themselves.*)

MRS. VOSKOVEC. Coming now with me into small room you most naughty boy.

(*They exit into the bathroom.*)

TATIANNA. Am fearing we bringing you much inconvenience.

MYLES. Well to tell you the truth…

(*He is interrupted by a series of high pitched Morse code sounds coming from the bathroom*)

MYLES. What in the world?

TATIANNA. Please no interference.

(*They come out of the bathroom.*)

MRS. VOSKOVEC. Punishment not possible in bathroom. Need more room to…get good swing. You have perhaps place outside with more room and unobstructed by mountains?

MYLES. Mesa, on top of the next hill, I guess.

(**MRS. VOSKOVEC** *looks to* **RIMSKY** *for approval.*)

RIMSKY. Is good.

MRS. VOSKOVEC. Is good. We return shortly.

(*The three of them exit.* **MYLES** *paces back and forth anxiously, goes over the ham radio but sees it is broken beyond repair.* **BLAINE** *walks in. He's covered in black smoke and his lab coat is almost burnt to a crisp.*)

MYLES. Blaine, am I glad to see you!

BLAINE. Let me guess. There's a cannonball and gunpowder stuck inside the telescope and you'd like me to climb inside it to remove them! Fine! When you think I'm down far enough, here's some matches to light the fuse!

MYLES. Will you settle down? There are some people here who aren't quite right.

BLAINE. There's at least one.

MYLES. I mean it, Blaine. I think they're foreign agents.

BLAINE. Foreign agents?

MYLES. They went to the top of the mesa to transmit a message over their radio.

BLAINE. What are you talking about?

MYLES. It may all fit together. Sputnik flying overhead. That strange hovering object captured on our photo. Three foreign agents portraying an average American family.

BLAINE. You must be wrong.

MYLES. You don't understand. They broke the phone and the ham set. And the university shuttle won't be back till morning to pick us up. Or whatever's left of us. Did you see my wife?

BLAINE. No. Wait, are you serious? Real foreign agents? If it's true... We have to protect Mrs. Stanton. We'll capture them.

MYLES. I'll make them wish they never came here. The main problem will be someone called Rimsky. Big fellow. You know the type. Tall, good looking, virile. It'll be almost like battling my own twin.

BLAINE. Let me take him.

MYLES. Imagine breaking off a steel support rod with your bare hands.

BLAINE. Let me take him to the back where you can jump him from behind.

MYLES. How are we going to overpower them?

BLAINE. We need some kind of weapon and we have nothing.

MYLES. Nothing? That's where I beg to differ with you. We have the very best weapons. Something that has been evolving for millions of years.

BLAINE. Clubs made out of wood?

MYLES. Our brains!

BLAINE. Can we kick around the clubs made out of wood idea a little more?

MYLES. We're going to outsmart them…Comrade Blaininsky. We use their life of secrecy to our advantage. Spies undercover can never be sure who's under the covers with them. Whether it's a harmless little teddy bear named Blaine or a steely nerved viper named Blaininsky who just happens to be their boss.

(MYLES sticks a cigarette in BLAINE's mouth and pulls up his collar. BLAINE spits out the cigarette and smoothes his collar back down.)

BLAINE. I'm leaving now.

(He backs up toward the door. MRS. VOSKOVEC, RIMSKY and TATIANNA walk in unseen by BLAINE.)

BLAINE. I'm going to hike down that road and notify the police. I only hope I do run into those three foreign agents. Because the way I feel right now I could lay them all out flat.

(He backs into RIMSKY and turns around.)

BLAINE. And give them nice relaxing massages. So you want to be first big fella?

(MRS. VOSKOVEC pulls out a gun.)

BLAINE. Right. Ladies first.

MRS. VOSKOVEC. Pleased to be moving back now.

TATIANNA. Our mission now placed in jeopardy.

MYLES. What are you going to do?

MRS. VOSKOVEC. Transmitting now for further instructions thank you. Rimsky, set up radio.

(RIMSKY exits outside. MRS. VOSKOVEC sees the luggage

on the floor and circles it)

MRS. VOSKOVEC. Why luggage?

BLAINE. It's...

MYLES. *(Quickly)* His. My assistant was going on a trip.

*(**TATIANNA** opens the luggage and pulls out a negligee.)*

TATIANNA. Am thinking he has gone too far already!

MYLES. Blaine! What is the meaning of this?

MRS. VOSKOVEC. In my country such behavior would not be tolerated.

MYLES. Obviously he has an illness. Or a syndrome. Don't worry, Blaine, I promise to stand by you.

*(**BLAINE** puts his arm around **MYLES**.)*

BLAINE. Thank you sir.

MYLES. Get away from me!

BLAINE. Yes sir.

MYLES. Well, off to the doctor. With any luck, they can cure you in time for next week's square dance.

BLAINE. Thank you, sir, I'd hate to invest any money in a dress I would only wear once.

*(**MYLES** and **BLAINE** move towards the door but their path is blocked by the **MRS. VOSKOVEC** who points her gun at them.)*

MRS. VOSKOVEC. Please to be moving back.

TATIANNA. Look! Strange man also has handcuffs in luggage.

MRS. VOSKOVEC. Handcuff them together.

*(**TATIANNA** does so, taking care to wrap the chain once around the arm of a desk chair. She acts drawn to **BLAINE**, not being to take her eyes off him.)*

MRS. VOSKOVEC. Join us outside when finishing while we await further instructions.

*(**MRS. VOSKOVEC** exits)*

TATIANNA. *(To* **BLAINE***)* Poor Babuska. Am understanding your confusion about wanting to wear women's clothing. Have brother like you back home.

BLAINE. *(Trying to move away from her)* That's nice.

TATIANNA. Perhaps would care to see his photograph?

BLAINE. I don't think so.

TATIANNA. Very handsome. Even in night gown.

BLAINE. No!

TATIANNA. No?

MYLES. What he means is, anybody can look good in a night gown. It's all a matter of lighting.

*(***TATIANNA** *takes a small photo out of her purse and shows it to* **BLAINE.***)*

BLAINE. And liquor.

*(***TATIANNA** *leaves.)*

MYLES. She might be our ticket out of here. Blaine, could you-

BLAINE. I'm *not* going out with her brother!

MYLES. You don't want to go out with my niece. You don't want to go out with her brother. Don't you like anybody?

*(***MRS. VOSKOVEC** *and* **TATIANNA** *reenter.)*

MRS. VOSKOVEC. Make sure strange man does not have key to handcuffs in pocket.

MYLES. He doesn't have the key.

TATIANNA. Found key.

*(***MRS. VOSKOVEC** *and* **TATIANNA** *exit.)*

MYLES. What was the key to my wife's handcuffs doing in your pocket?

BLAINE. I'm studying to be a locksmith?

MYLES. But why do you have the one and only key that would fit in my wife's one and only set of handcuffs?

BLAINE. I took it out of the luggage when you weren't looking so I could make another copy in case she lost her own key?

MYLES. But why…

BLAINE. I'm in love with your wife! We were going to elope after you got your divorce!

(Pause.)

Sir.

MYLES. *(Barely controlling himself)* My wife…my assistant…handcuffs…

(**MYLES** *begins moving towards* **BLAINE**, *who does his best to keep the chair they are both handcuffed to between himself and* **MYLES** *as they move across the floor.*)

MYLES. I'm going to kill you now, Blaine.

BLAINE. Couldn't you think of it as now you'll be able to spend more time in the observatory?

MYLES. Oh, so you're doing me a favor! Well it's my turn to do you a favor! I'm going to kill you before you have to meet her mother. I know it doesn't sound like much now, but believe me, you're making out!

BLAINE. I know how you feel sir, but killing me won't bring your wife back to you.

MYLES. You're right. I can't keep her chained to me. My luck, I can keep you chained to me, but not her! I guess I can't blame you for the fact she doesn't love me.

BLAINE. I never met to hurt you, sir. It just happened. We may never get out of this alive, but if we do…

MYLES. Yes?

BLAINE. Could you tell me what you think your wife might like for her birthday? It's coming up and she's so hard to shop for.

(**MYLES** *moves threateningly towards* **BLAINE** *but stops suddenly.*)

MYLES. My wife's birthday is coming up? I forgot all about it. If I weren't going to die now she'd kill me. I guess she's ending up with the right guy after all. Maybe she was right about me.

BLAINE. I wish there was something I could say.

MYLES. Save your pity mister! We Stantons are made of sterner stuff. *(Trying to be brave)* I suppose there are a few things you should know about her. She likes to eat at Vinnie's Pizzeria on Sundays. Don't let her order the Tiramisu. You'll spend the rest of the week reassuring her she's not getting fat.

BLAINE. I'll remember that.

MYLES. And she likes hanging her nylons in the bathroom. Don't bother arguing with her about it. You'll lose.

BLAINE. I'll keep that in mind.

MYLES. And she often gets an itch on her lower back she can't reach to scratch.

BLAINE. I'll scratch it for her.

MYLES. *(Angry)* You'll *buy* her a backscratcher! Not that any of that matters anymore.

BLAINE. Then you think it's over for us?

MYLES. Over for us? Not by a long shot! Not when I have a plan.

BLAINE. A plan? You have a plan?

MYLES. I have a plan.

BLAINE. *(Yelling)* COMRADE RIMSKY! HELP!

*(While **BLAINE** struggles to free himself from the handcuffs, **MYLES** uses his other hand to cover **BLAINE**'s mouth.)*

MYLES. Shhhhh! I tell you this one can't miss. It'll knock you out!

*(**BLAINE** removes **MYLES** hand from over his mouth and pushes him back violently. **MYLES** falls down, knocking his head against the control panel.)*

BLAINE. Dr. Stanton. Dr. Stanton, are you ok? Dr. Stanton, speak to me.

*(He tries to rouse **MYLES** but without success.)*

BLAINE. He's...he's dead. I've killed Dr. Stanton. You

know, I think I have to leave this whole last year off my resume.

(BLACKOUT)

End of Scene II

Scene III

(AT RISE: Minutes later. **MRS. VOSKOVEC** *and* **RIMSKY** *reenter the Observatory through the front door.* **MYLES** *is sprawled out on the floor and* **BLAINE** *is coolly sitting down next to him smoking a cigarette.)*

MRS. VOSKOVEC. What has been happening?

BLAINE. I've been doing your job for you. Idiots! How such fools could have been sent on such a delicate assignment is beyond me. Heads will roll. Beginning with yours if you do not release me at once!

MRS. VOSKOVEC. Am I to be understanding you killed him? Your employer?

BLAINE. My employer? This dog!

*(***BLAINE*** slaps* **MYLES.***)*

BLAINE. This pig!

*(***BLAINE*** kicks* **MYLES.***)*

BLAINE. This cheapskate!

*(***BLAINE*** tweaks* **MYLES** *nose.)*

BLAINE. His death was of little consequence anyway. He was marked for elimination soon enough. His photographer accidentally caught my craft on his camera. Release me!

MRS. VOSKOVEC. Un-handcuff him.

RIMSKY. Is only poor attempt to save own life.

*(***RIMSKY*** takes off* **BLAINE***'s handcuffs.)*

MRS. VOSKOVEC. So, you say you too are undercovers.

BLAINE. Undercovers? I've got so many covers I sleep with the windows open.

MRS. VOSKOVEC. All I am wishing to know.

(In a flash, **RIMSKY** *wrestles* **BLAINE** *to the floor and* **MRS. VOSKOVEC** *a.k.a.* **AGENT LAWSON** *takes a small walkie-talkie our of her pocket. Her voice is now urgent without a trace of accent.)*

AGENT LAWSON. Red dog! Red dog! Over! Have Sparrow in custody. All units report in.

BLAINE. What? What happened to your accents?

(**RIMSKY** a.k.a. **AGENT MALCOLM**, slams **BLAINE** into a chair)

AGENT MALCOLM. We can drop them now. Just like we're gonna drop you in the hot seat, Comrade.

BLAINE. Hot seat? You mean electric chair?

AGENT MALCOLM. I'm talking about an all expense paid trip up the river, free accommodations at the gray bar motel, last meal of your choice followed by all the juice we can pump into you.

BLAINE. That's a relief. I thought I was in trouble.

AGENT LAWSON. Trouble? Our juice doesn't come out of little round oranges.

AGENT MALCOLM. We're talking 25,000 volts courtesy of Uncle Sam.

BLAINE. But I haven't done anything. I thought you were spies. I was only pretending to be one long enough to escape.

AGENT LAWSON. And that's why you killed Dr. Stanton.

BLAINE. It was an accident.

AGENT MALCOLM. How convenient the only one to back up your story is dead. Face it, you change your story more often than I change my socks. Both stink and no judge is going to buy either.

BLAINE. But I tell you I'm not a spy. And will you please move your feet?

AGENT LAWSON. Funny, how nobody's a spy after they're caught. Now talk!

BLAINE. This can't be happening. It just can't be. My mind must be playing tricks on me.

AGENT MALCOLM. Yes the mind can pay tricks on you. For instance, my finger sometimes looks just like a finger. But at other times it can look like a lethal weapon that can crash through a man's eye socket, penetrate his brain and kill him before he hits the ground.

(**BLAINE** *looks closely at* **AGENT MALCOLM**'s *finger.*)

BLAINE. Must be rough on your manicurist.

AGENT LAWSON. Quit stalling. Who's your control agent?

MALCOLM. Maybe a session with a thumbscrew will help.

AGENT LAWSON. Our thumbscrew?

(**MALCOLM** *and* **AGENT LAWSON** *draw close together with a strange intense passion. Then just as quickly take a deep breath and regain their composure.*)

BLAINE. Thumbscrew?

LAWSON. Agent Malcolm, I told you we can't use that on… private citizens. We serve at the direction of the Chief of Intelligence.

MALCOLM. If you don't mind I serve something a little older and a little more revered. Sure it's wrinkled, yellowed and worn around the edges but year after year it continues to work.

LAWSON. The Constitution?

MALCOLM. Actually I was talking about Grandma. She's still paying off my tuition and helping with my mortgage. And I'd hate to see her hard earned money be wasted in a world that makes it safe for commies and reds like him to get away with undermining our way of life.

BLAINE. I'm not undermining anything. Why won't you believe me?

AGENT MALCOLM. Because I believe in Johnny Little League instead.

BLAINE. But I've never even heard of him.

AGENT MALCOLM. I'd be surprised if you had. He's little freckle faced boy coming home from a game of baseball expecting to find a glass of milk and cookies waiting for him. But instead he finds a glass of vodka and a plate of borscht. He wonders what could have happened in the few hours he was gone.

MYLES. And if dinner consists of vodka, borscht and turnips they may have done him the biggest favor of his life.

BLAINE. Dr. Stanton, you're alive!

AGENT LAWSON. What's going on here?

BLAINE. I couldn't feel your pulse. I'd given you up for dead.

MYLES. Well, on behalf of all your future patients, thank you for choosing astronomy over medicine.

BLAINE. Oh really? Just by the way, if you're keeping score, that plan you had about me being a spy? It laid an egg. And as scrambled and half-baked as all your others.

MYLES. At least *I* get an idea now and then. Just who are guys?

BLAINE. Federal Agents. Careful of the big one. Said he can drive his finger through an eye socket until it penetrated the brain. I'd pay money to see him put on a pair of contacts.

AGENT MALCOLM. Pipe down. Special Agent Lawson, we may have made a slight mistake with these two.

AGENT LAWSON. Let's not sugarcoat it, Special Agent Malcolm. This is a premature contact forced by random circumstance outside the purview of established policy guidelines.

BLAINE. All that training and they can't spell screw-up?

(**AGENT MALCOLM** *goes on walkie-talkie.*)

AGENT MALCOLM. Unit one. Unit one. Hold position. Sparrow still in custody but may not be able to pluck him.

BLAINE. He did say, "pluck"?

MYLES. Who's Sparrow?

AGENT LAWSON. Code name for your assistant. Welcome to Operation Aviary, Dr. Stanton. Our attempt to discover the source of coded transmissions through the airwaves. We've had all of you under surveillance for the past several months.

MYLES. That is outrageous, unacceptable behavior! My congressman is going to hear about this!

(Pause.)

What's my code name?

AGENT MALCOLM. Dodo.

MYLES. My congressman is indeed going to hear about this! However, I'll probably leave out the part about my code name.

(Pause.)

Dodo?

AGENT MALCOLM. Dodo: A large flightless and dull-witted bird forced to extinction because it could not adapt to its changing environment.

MYLES. I know what a dodo is!

BLAINE. I'm Sparrow.

AGENT LAWSON. Enough! What was that craft your assistant was talking about that was accidentally captured by your photographer?

BLAINE. When I thought you were spies, I didn't have any code-word or proof that I could use to make believe I was one too. So to buy time I took a gamble that the third nipple of Virgo was some kind of craft used by secret agents.

MYLES. Say, that's very good, Blaine.

*(**BLAINE** pull **MYLES** aside.)*

BLAINE. Then that light *is* some kind of craft.

MYLES. But whose? And from what country?

BLAINE. Or from which world?

*(**AGENT MALCOLM** walks back inside.)*

AGENT MALCOLM. If these two are telling the truth...

AGENT LAWSON. Then who is sending those transmissions.

AGENT MALCOLM. You know it leaves only one other possibility.

AGENT LAWSON. Falcon.

MYLES. Who the hell is Falcon?

AGENT LAWSON. Your wife, Dr. Stanton. Your wife.

MYLES. What?! First of all, suspecting my wife of treason is ridiculous. And second of all, why does she get a nice code name like Falcon and I'm stuck with Dodo?

AGENT LAWSON. Don't take it personally, Dr. Stanton. We assigned code names based on the degree of perceived threat, not inherent intellectual capabilities.

MYLES. Oh. Well...that's better.

(As soon as **MYLES** *turns away,* **AGENTS LAWSON** *and* **MALCOLM** *look at each other and giggle.)*

MYLES. But I still refuse to believe my pussycat, Hali Barbinsky Stravonovich is a spy!

(They all stare at **MYLES.***)*

MYLES. Well what are you looking at? So what? My last name is Stanton. It's English. My ancestors burned down Washington in the war of 1812. Does that make me a threat to national security?

*(***AGENT MALCOLM** *is writing in a little book.)*

AGENT MALCOLM. That's two "T"s in Stanton?

MYLES. She's my wife. If she were a spy that would mean either I was a spy too or...You're gonna laugh, the biggest idiot who ever lived on the face of this planet! Ha, ha, ha!

(The **AGENTS** *just stare at him.)*

MYLES. Why'd I think you'd laugh?

AGENT LAWSON. Time may be running short. Coded transmissions from this area have increased over the past few days. Is it a coincidence that Sputnik is orbiting just as your wife is preparing to leave the area?

MYLES. If you're looking for a real mystery to solve try to figure out what she sees in her new fiancée. But Hali as a spy...Never.

AGENT MALCOLM. There may be a way to find out if which one of us is wrong.

AGENT LAWSON. Permit us to give you an injection to probe your subconscious. There may be some incident or event you either didn't note at the time or simply pushed out of your mind in order to live with it. Let us find out. Of course we can't force you to take this injection.

(**MYLES** *rolls up his sleeves and* **AGENT LAWSON** *prepares the injection.*)

MYLES. Fine! Let's clear this up. Oh, if I start to say anything about a night where I dressed up as the sheriff of Dodge City and Hali dressed up as the saloon keeper and I showed her my quick draw...

AGENT LAWSON. Don't worry. We'll try to keep the giggling down.

(**AGENT LAWSON** *lays* **MYLES** *down on the cot.*)

AGENT MALCOLM. Our department doesn't pass judgement on an individual's private behavior, however deviant or perverse.

MYLES. That's good to hear.

AGENT LAWSON. That department is in another building.

AGENT MALCOLM. As long as your behavior doesn't affect the security of the United States, you have nothing to fear from us.

MYLES. Does that include the time where I dressed up as a German U-boat commander and I found Hali floating on a raft and I showed how quickly I could fire my torpedoes?

AGENT LAWSON. Goodnight, Dr. Stanton.

(**AGENT LAWSON** *injects him.*)

MYLES. ...And my torpedo exploded before it hit its target...I just want you to know...Lots of pressure in the office...Zzzzz.

(*BLACKOUT*)

End of Scene III

Scene IV

(AT RISE: Lapse of time of only a few minutes. **AGENTS LAWSON** *and* **MALCOLM** *are seated by the cot where the "figure" of* **MYLES** *lies stretched out cold in front of them, head turned away from the audience. Blue and red soft spotlights illuminate only the center of the stage where there is now a small kitchen table, with a checkerboard tablecloth.)*

AGENT LAWSON. All right, Dr. Stanton. Go back in time to the morning of July 12th, the day we intercepted the first coded transmissions from the area. What happened that morning between you and your wife before you left for work? Don't leave out anything.

*(***MYLES** *enters from stage left and* **HALI** *enters from stage right and seat themselves at the kitchen table.)*

MYLES. Where's the bacon?

HALI. You eat too much bacon.

MYLES. But I like bacon.

HALI. But it's not good for you.

MYLES. But I like bacon.

HALI. But it's not good for you.

MYLES. But I like bacon.

AGENT LAWSON. Dr. Stanton!

*(***MYLES** *and* **HALI** *freeze on stage.)*

AGENT LAWSON. Let's move forward in time a couple of minutes. Proceed.

*(***MYLES** *and* **HALI** *unfreeze.)*

MYLES. But I like bacon.

HALI. But it's not good for you.

MYLES. But I like bacon.

AGENT LAWSON. Dr. Stanton!

*(***MYLES** *and* **HALI** *freeze.)*

AGENT LAWSON. Listen…Let's go to that part of the

morning after you and your wife were done arguing about the damn bacon!

(MYLES and HALI unfreeze.)

MYLES. I'm sorry, Pussycat. I know you're just looking after me.

HALI. Because I love you.

MYLES. And I love you. Say…there's pits in my orange juice.

HALI. There are no pits in your orange juice.

MYLES. There are too pits in my orange juice.

HALI. There are no pits in your orange juice.

MYLES. There are…

AGENT LAWSON. Dr. Stanton!

(MYLES and HALI freeze.)

AGENT LAWSON. Dr. Stanton. I want you to listen carefully. Breakfast is over! You are preparing to go to work now. What is happening?

(MYLES and HALI unfreeze.)

MYLES. Pussycat, I have to go to work. What are you up to today?

HALI. Oh, the usual things. Hairdresser, shopping, PTA.

MYLES. *(Hugging her)* What a wonderful wife. Attending PTA meetings when we don't even have any kids.

HALI. I think it's important to prepare myself for any eventuality.

MYLES. You're telling me. But you've got a lot to learn about knitting before starting on baby booties.

HALI. What do you mean?

(MYLES walks over to the end of the stage and brings back a black knit cap and sweater.)

MYLES. These will never fit a baby!

HALI. Where did you find those?

MYLES. Behind the water-heater. You can't keep secrets from me. Wait, you're not already…

HALI. No, no. Just practicing for that happy, happy eventuality. You said it was time for you to go to work?

(She starts pushing him out the "door".)

MYLES. I'm so lucky to have you. I'd like to broadcast it to the whole world. Which I should be able to do when you finally finish that radio you've been building.

(She pulls him back.)

HALI. What radio?

MYLES. The one you're keeping in the basement behind the loose brick.

HALI. I can explain that, Myles...

MYLES. So you're learning radio repair on the side to earn a little extra for our family. I understand. I'm a modern man, my wife can work.

*(**MYLES** pantomimes opening a window.)*

MYLES. Do you hear that world!?! I'm the luckiest man who ever lived! Me and Uncle Boris! He phoned yesterday. I didn't even know you had an Uncle Boris.

*(**HALI** pantomimes shutting the window.)*

HALI. Myles. In the last few minutes, we've talked about my attending PTA meetings when we have no children, a black cap, a radio, and Uncle Boris. Anything strike you strange about this morning?

MYLES. There are raisins in the muffins. I wasn't going to bring that up. I don't like raisins in my muffins.

HALI. I'll try to remember that in the future.

MYLES. Off to work, then. What a drive. You know, I think I'm going to deduct that new car hi-fi I bought on my taxes as a business expense. I'll just say it's equipment for the observatory.

HALI. Is that legal?

MYLES. No. But I've got a burnt out light bulb in the garage that's a lot brighter than the people who work for the government.

BLAINE. Uh, Dr. Stanton...

MYLES. I mean I think they'd starve to death if they didn't have the government to employ them.

BLAINE. Wake up Dr. Stanton.

MYLES. I think they're just a bunch of clock watchers and doughnut dippers. Me worry about a little creative bookkeeping? I don't think so.

BLAINE. *(Yelling)* DR. STANTON!

(Lights go to black. They fade up showing **HALI** *gone and* **MYLES** *lying on the cot in front of a frowning* **AGENT LAWSON** *and* **AGENT MALCOLM.***)*

MYLES. Is it over? I'm glad we cleared that up. Now when can I expect that apology?

AGENT LAWSON. Well, provided you're still able to scare up a dime after our audit, phone us and we'll discuss it.

MYLES. Audit?

BLAINE. Don't you remember anything you said?

MYLES. No. I mean everything is ok with Hali, right? Isn't it?

(All three of them quietly turn their back on **MYLES** *and slowly walk away.)*

MYLES. Hey fellas...tell me everything is all right. Com'on, we can all take Zippy the dog for a walk now.

AGENT LAWSON. Dr. Stanton. I'm sorry. Everything you recollected under the influence of the serum only works to verify our original suspicions.

AGENT MALCOLM. And, we believe, the fact that she wants to divorce you at this particular moment has less to do with you and the fact that you are impossible to live with than it is a desperate attempt to establish another cover with someone else in a different location.

MYLES. Ah ha! So, Blaine has been behind it all along.

(The teo agents gasp.)

BLAINE. What?

MYLES. Sending out applications to different observatories behind my back. What other nefarious secret deeds were you up to here, Sparrow?

BLAINE. You're just jealous because Hali happens to prefer my company to yours, Dodo.

MYLES. Dodo!

*(**BLAINE** and **MYLES** begin wrestling each other. **AGENT MALCOLM** breaks it up.)*

AGENT LAWSON. That's enough. Why does she want to leave now? Why does she want you to get a job elsewhere?

BLAINE. I don't know.

AGENT LAWSON. Does she love you? Or just need you to escape?

BLAINE. She's no spy! You're wrong. All of you wrong!

AGENT MALCOLM. Face it! Your story has more holes in it than my woolen underwear and any jury will be able to see through both.

BLAINE. I think the only break I've got is I won't be on the jury.

AGENT LAWSON. Your only chance is if you agree to taking the serum.

BLAINE. Serum!? I know my rights. Give me one good reason why I should?

*(**AGENT MALCOLM** extends his forefinger and holds it menacingly in front of **BLAINE**S eye.)*

BLAINE. I had to ask.

AGENT LAWSON. Roll up your sleeve.

*(**AGENT LAWSON** injects **BLAINE**. **BLAINE** lays back on the cot. The lights fade to black and come up dim. The "Figure" of **BLAINE** can be seen lying on the cot. blue and green soft lights illuminate the center of the stage, and a small kitchen table with a checkerboard tablecloth.)*

AGENT LAWSON. Alright. It is still the morning of July 12.

*(A knock on a door can be heard. **HALI** comes from stage right, crosses over and escorts a slightly nervous **BLAINE** to center stage by the table.)*

BLAINE. I still feel funny still doing this behind his back.
HALI. It's better this way. We don't need any complications.
BLAINE. Muffins with raisins! You've made my favorite!

(BLAINE takes a bite, then suddenly drops the muffin and staggers back, grabbing his throat.)

BLAINE. HELP! I can't breathe…I'm choking…
AGENT LAWSON. Dr. Stanton! Will you please take your hands off your assistant's throat!
MYLES. I was just straightening his collar.

(MYLES removes his hands from around the throat of the "figure" lying on the cot. BLAINE, slowly straightens up)

BLAINE. Whew! Say, how about some bacon?
HALI. Of course.

(In a fit of anger MYLES tries to leap on the "figure," lying on the cot, but is restrained by AGENTS LAWSON and MALCOLM. They quickly tie and gag HIM in the chair as HALI prepares the bacon)

BLAINE. I've sent applications for employment to several other observatories.
HALI. I know you'll be hired. You're the best, baby.
BLAINE. I'm especially proud of my last paper, "*The Movement of Hydrogen Clouds in the Galaxy: An Important Phenomenon or Just Passing Gas.*"

(HALI pushes BLAINE passionately on top of the kitchen table, and climbs on him.)

HALI. I wasn't talking about astronomy. The only stars I see come out when I'm with you.
BLAINE. Me too. But I think it's because I'm sitting on a fork.
HALI. Have you ever done it on the kitchen table, Blaine? Take me now.
BLAINE. Right now?
HALI. Don't let me lose the moment.
BLAINE. Okie Dokie.

(**BLAINE** *struggles awkwardly to hold* **HALI** *in an intimate embrace trying to stay on top of the kitchen table, accidentally knocking everything off it.*)

BLAINE. I wish that cheap husband of yours would have bought a bigger table. Whoops, there goes the butter. Watch the jam. Perhaps if we... Was that syrup? How does Dr. Stanton eat such a big breakfast and get any work done?

HALI. Blaine, I'm losing the moment.

BLAINE. Roger Wilco.

HALI. Blaine, I just lost the moment.

BLAINE. I just lost my glasses.

HALI. Oh Blaine. It doesn't matter. Promise you'll do things for me, Blaine. For me. To me. But mainly for me.

BLAINE. I promise. It's a big wonderful world beyond this kitchen table. I'll work so hard to make you happy in it. Except I doubt that we can move out of here by October 7th.

HALI. (*Unpleasantly surprised*) What?

BLAINE. What's the difference as long as you have your Blainey-Pooh?

(*Still on the kitchen table* **HALI** *quickly moves on top of* **BLAINE**, *and threateningly holds him by the collar.*)

HALI. I told you it was important for us to leave by October 7th. Are you rejecting me? I don't take rejection well. It makes me want to hurt the people I think are hurting me.

(*She picks up a knife.*)

HALI. We're a team now. Just like this bread and jelly. Where the one goes, the other must follow.

(*She slowly and carefully scrapes the side of his cheek with the knife and wipes it on a piece of bread and takes a bite out of it.*)

BLAINE. I promise we'll be out by October 7th. Even if I have to get a job in a filling station.

HALI. Thank you, Blaine. It won't be so bad getting a job during the day. That would leave the nights to us.

BLAINE. Just me, you and the knife in the dark? Great. But could we leave just one light on. I may be the jelly, but I'm in no hurry to find out if I'm raspberry or cherry flavored.

*(Fade to black and then come up again a few moments later. The kitchen table and **HALI** are gone.)*

AGENT LAWSON. *(To **AGENT MALCOLM**)* Untie Dr. Stanton... But uh, save the rope and gag.

*(**AGENTS MALCOLM** and **LAWSON** draw close to each other with an intense passion then just as quickly take a deep breath and regain their composer. **AGENT MALCOLM** unties **MYLES**. **BLAINE** slowly comes out of his sleep. He sees a disappointed **MYLES** quietly walk away.)*

BLAINE. Dr. Stanton. Dr. Stanton, please.

*(**MYLES** ignores him and looks very depressed. **AGENTS LAWSON** and **MALCOLM** observe the effect the session has had on **MYLES** and after a quick conference **AGENT MALCOLM** approaches **MYLES**.)*

AGENT MALCOLM. Dr. Stanton. I've just had a conference with Agent Lawson and we've both agreed that as of now you have a new code name. Goodbye Dodo. Welcome aboard, Turkey.

*(**AGENT LAWSON** elbows **AGENT MALCOLM**.)*

AGENT MALCOLM. I mean, Eagle.

MYLES. I thought you assigned code names based on perceived threat?

AGENT MALCOLM. Do you want the new code name or not?

MYLES. I'll take it. I'll take it. But you...Blaine...

AGENT LAWSON. Right now Falcon is under the watchful eyes of Agent Brice.

*(**TATIANNA** a.k.a. **AGENT BRICE**, stumbles in unseen through the front door, dizzy and holding her hand to her head.)*

AGENT LAWSON. *(Continued)* Yes, eyes that never close.

(SHE bumps into the wall)

And always on her toes.

(SHE lays down)

The scent of the prey in her nose.

(SHE Sneezes)

(Turning around) Agent Brice!

(They all run to her side)

AGENT LAWSON. *(Continued)* What happened? Where's Falcon?

AGENT BRICE. I don't know. I lost her when she went behind the generator shed. Then somebody hit me from behind.

BLAINE. Can I get you a glass of water?

AGENT BRICE. *(Smiling)* Sparrow.

MYLES. Can I get you some aspirin?

AGENT BRICE. Dodo.

MYLES. I guess there must be a hold-up on the paper work. I'm known as Eagle now.

AGENT BRICE. You have the same code name as the Admiral's Fox Terrier?

MYLES. Huh?

AGENT LAWSON. *(Nudging her)* No, no, no. We're redoing all code names.

AGENT BRICE. Oh. Sure.

AGENT LAWSON. Unfortunately, Falcon may now have the advantage

*(The walkie-talkie in **AGENT LAWSON**'s coat begins to beep)*

AGENT LAWSON. Unit Two here, over. Right. Falcon located and in the air. Stay back. We'll be ready.

*(**AGENT LAWSON** puts away walkie-talkie)*

AGENT LAWSON. *(Continued)* You're wife is on the way back.

In less than 20 minutes Sputnik will be directly over us. We want to know the tie-in between that and you wife's desperate attempt to leave under a new cover. We want you to have her lead us to Uncle Boris. Carry this homing device and microphone on you. You may feel safer if you take this gun.

MYLES. A gun?

AGENT LAWSON. Now remember, Dr. Stanton. Your wife is a professional. If you let sentiment interfere with your judgement, we may not be able to help you.

MYLES. Where will you be?

AGENT LAWSON. Almost close enough to touch.

(**AGENT LAWSON** checks her gun)

AGENT LAWSON. *(Continued)* I know this has been rough for you, Eagle. You've been the unwitting pawn in a game of international chess. The clown in the carnival high-diving into a bucket of water just before it gets replaced by a damp sponge. The –

MYLES. I think we've pretty much established who I am.

AGENT LAWSON. *(Smiling)* Right. But you're one more thing also. And I hope I'm not being out of line. You're a person I want to buy a breakfast for when this is over, Dr. Stanton. Or… Or can I call you Myles?

MYLES. Breakfast? With bacon, too? Muffins and no raisins?

AGENT LAWSON. Yeah, yeah, bacon too. Muffins hold the raisins. Orange juice strained no seeds. Got ya. Here's your walkie-talkie. Goodbye.

(**LAWSON, BRICE & MALCOLM** *head toward the door*)

AGENT LAWSON. We'd better get out of here quick, before I decide to throw in with his wife.

(BLACKOUT)

End of Scene Iv

Scene V

AT RISE: Only a few moments have lapsed.

MYLES *is playing with the gun, pretending to shoot things.* **BLAINE** *keeps walking up to him looking for something to say, but nervously backs off at the last moment, as* **MYLES** *continues to mow down imaginary targets. It is not until he puts his gun away that* **BLAINE** *finally finds the courage to engage his attention while putting on a new lab coat.*

BLAINE. Hard to believe this is my last lab coat.

(Pause)

I don't know how I'm going to get home with no gas in my car.

(Pause)

It sure is amazing they can fit a microphone inside these little earrings.

MYLES. Look, I know we have to speak to each other, but I don't want you talking to me. How could you have made love to my wife on my kitchen table!

BLAINE. I never made love to your wife. Not really.

MYLES. Blaine, the only reason I'm not going to tear you limb from limb is because that's *my* lab coat you're wearing and right now my government is depending on me.

*(***MYLES** *leans back on his chair and tips over doing a backwards somersault. HE quickly takes out his walkie-talkie and turns it on)*

MYLES. *(Continued)* Eagle ok, repeat, Eagle ok. All units hold position. Eagle alive and well. Do you copy?

MALCOLM *(Over radio)* Get off the radio you idiot!

MYLES. Copy that. Over and Out. Well, the walkie-talkie works.

BLAINE. I think they're wrong about her.

MYLES. We were all wrong about her. Hali was smooth. Slick on the outside but full of holes on the inside like a piece of Swiss cheese. And I followed her like a lab mouse running through a maze. A maze built out of lies and deceit where the payoff at the end is an empty feeling in the pit of your stomach that leaves a bitter taste in your mouth. Yeah, that's me. Myles the mouse. Well, it may be too late for some of us, but not for others.

(**MYLES** *walks up to the Hamster cage*)

MYLES. *(Continued)* I know how you feel Toby. We're two of a kind, you and me. And today I think we've both earned our freedom.

(**MYLES** *takes the cage and walks over to the door and opens the cage*)

MYLES. Look. Hali could learn something from him. He, at least, doesn't want to leave me.

BLAINE. He's still glued to the side of the cage sir.

MYLES. Oh.

(*After a brief struggle,* **MYLES** *frees the hamster from the side of the cage*)

MYLES. There you go old friend. I know it's difficult to say goodbye. But if you don't look back…

BLAINE. He's gone sir.

(**MYLES** *and* **BLAINE** *are both looking out the window*)

MYLES. Oh. I see. Boy, look at him run. WHAT, YOU'RE LATE FOR A DATE AT THE THEATER?!

BLAINE. Easy sir, easy.

MYLES. I'm ok, I'm ok. And he'll be ok, too. Soon, he'll meet other hamsters. Life goes on doesn't it? Say, are hamsters desert creatures?

(*A coyote howls in the distance*)

BLAINE. Hmmm… Not any more. But coyotes sure have adapted well.

(*The radio beeps.* **MYLES** *takes the walkie talkie out of his pocket*)

LAWSON *(Over Radio)* Falcon will arrive in one minute.

MYLES. We've got to look busy. What was the last thing we were we doing before she left?

BLAINE. Pulling cactus needles out of my body.

MYLES. Quit trying to cheer me up.

BLAINE. And we were working on the telescope.

MYLES. Right. Now remember. No slip ups.

(**MYLES** and **BLAINE** pickup some tools and start hammering and making a lot of noise. **HALI** walks in)

HALI. All right, Myles, I'm back. Let's get going.

MYLES. Sure thing, Falcon.

(**BLAINE** hits **MYLES** on the foot with a hammer)

MYLES (Continued) I mean pussycat. What kept you?

HALI. Oh a little trouble with the... car. Shall we go? Perhaps we could pick up something to eat on the way.

MYLES. That sounds good. Maybe have a little wine with our dinner. I suppose you prefer... *RED!*

(**BLAINE** hits **MYLES** in the foot with the hammer again)

HALI. I don't drink at all. You know that.

MYLES. Of course, of course. We've lived together, and you'd think I'd know *all* about you by now.

HALI. What's wrong with you Myles? Your eye is twitching.

MYLES. Really? How interesting. Maybe there's a *FOREIGN AGENT* in it.

(**BLAINE** hits **MYLES** in the foot with the hammer one more time. **MYLES** grabs the hammer and chases **BLAINE** with it while **HALI**'s back is turned)

HALI. Myles, you sound like you're coming unglued.

(**HALI** sees the empty hamster cage)

HALI. (Continued) Speaking of which, where's Toby?

MYLES. Well, for *your* information moving faster than ever before!

HALI. Myles, I wish you'd leave that poor hamster alone.

MYLES. I don't think that will be a problem anymore either.

HALI. Look Myles, I don't want to fight. Let's just get going.

(**MYLES** *picks up a wrench*)

MYLES. *(Continued)* Let me get this bolt tightened, and I'll go to the bathroom and we'll be on our way.

HALI. Fine.

BLAINE. Would you like me to put your luggage in the car darling?

(**MYLES** *hits* **BLAINE** *on the foot with his wrench*)

BLAINE. I mean Hali.

(**MYLES** *hits* **BLAINE** *on the foot with his wrench again*)

BLAINE. I mean Mrs. Stanton.

HALI. *(Impatiently)* Yes, yes, yes.

(**MYLES** *goes into the bathroom and* **HALI** *immediately tears the luggage from* **BLAINE***'s hands and pushes HIM in a chair, sits on top of HIS lap and passionately runs HER fingers through his hair*)

HALI. *(Continued)* Miss me?

BLAINE. *(Panicky)* Pussycat, please!

HALI. Oh Blaine, you make it exciting! So dangerous! Come on. Right now while Myles is in the bathroom!

BLAINE. Are you crazy?

HALI. Don't worry. Myles has never left the bathroom in under five minutes. Do you know what we can do in five minutes?

BLAINE. Make out our wills?

HALI. Blaine, I'm starting to feel rejected again.

BLAINE. Uh-oh.

(*SHE undoes his tie and wraps it around his neck, slowly pulling it tight*)

HALI. Say something nice.

(SHE continues to pull on the necktie)

BLAINE. You're... taking... my... breath... away.

(SHE removes the necktie)

HALI. That's better. Remember, you're to leave the observatory immediately after us. Meet me at the Drifting Sands Motel.

BLAINE. Right. I just have to pick up a few things first. Some soap, toothpaste, maybe those new clip-on ties...

HALI. Just don't be late.

BLAINE. I've got a surprise for you. But you have to get off my lap first.

*(**HALI** reluctantly gets off **BLAINE** who goes over to the desk and hands her a small box. SHE opens it and removes the earrings)*

HALI. They're lovely, Blaine, but they don't match anything I own.

BLAINE. I want you to wear them now. As a going away present.

(He clumsily puts the earrings on her)

BLAINE. Beautiful.

HALI. *(While nibbling on his ear)* Maybe you can write them off your taxes like you did the bracelet you bought me. You can call these ear aids, and make it a medical deduction.

BLAINE. *(Loudly, and into her earrings)* I'm shocked you could ever think of such a thing! I am proud to pay my taxes to the fine people who run the government!

HALI. Blaine, you don't have to shout.

BLAINE. Sorry.

*(The door to the bathroom begins to open and as **BLAINE** bends down to pick up the luggage, **MYLES** comes out of the bathroom)*

HALI. Myles will you help him. I'll be out in a second.

*(**HALI** goes into the bathroom)*

MYLES. I don't know how to keep her here.

BLAINE. At least she's wearing the earrings. I wish I knew where those agents were. I'll put this luggage in the car and look around.

(**BLAINE** *exits and* **HALI** *comes out of the bathroom*)

MYLES. Interesting that in less than a few minutes that Sputnik will be directly over us.

HALI. We really have to leave, Myles.

MYLES. What's the hurry? Perhaps we can catch a glimpse of it.

HALI. Goodbye, Myles. I'll have the lawyer mail you the copy of the divorce.

(**MYLES** *pulls out his gun*)

HALI. *(Continued)* A gun? What game are we supposed to be playing now, Myles? Are you supposed to be the tough gangster on the lam and I'm the meek librarian you take hostage?

MYLES. This time it's no game, Hali.

(Pause)

But if it were, how would that one work again?

HALI. What's wrong, Myles?

MYLES. What's wrong? I know all about you, that's what's wrong! I could forgive you about Blaine. But not for selling out your country. I can't let you leave.

HALI. I see. And now you propose to use that gun on me?

MYLES. Hardly. I'm not going to make it that easy for either of us. This gun is for you.

(**MYLES** *throws her the gun*)

MYLES. *(Continued)* If you want to leave you'll have to shoot me.

HALI. And you think I won't?

MYLES. I think everything costs in the end, but I won't pick up the tab for you on this one, honey. Oh sure, the bullets are paid for but it won't be until you shoot that you discover exactly what it was you bought. Because all sales are final and you can't return the merchandise. A corpse is a messy thing. It's damaged goods you can't unload in the final minutes of a yard sale.

HALI. I'd be impressed, Myles, except it all boils down to the same thing. If there's a killing to be done, let Hali do it. Just like if there's a meal to be cooked or a shirt to be ironed let Hali do it. You're not being brave, you just don't want to take the responsibility for doing anything. What did you want out of marriage Myles? Sorry, but I'm not a janitor, Myles. Not for your home. Not for your life.

(SHE throws him the gun)

A 45 can handle a lot of things. All the things the man standing behind it can't.

(BLAINE walks in)

BLAINE. Luggage is aboard.

(MYLES turns and points the gun at BLAINE)

BLAINE. *(Continued)* Ok, ok and I siphoned out a gallon of gas too.

MYLES. Never mind that. You better go outside and find the agents.

BLAINE. Oh. Right.

HALI. Just be sure they are federal agents before you find them.

MYLES. What?

HALI. Are you sure you know which one of us works for the government?

MYLES. You're great at games Hali, but this is too clumsy.

BLAINE. Is it possible then?

MYLES. No, no, no, no, no!

(Pause)

Think so?

BLAINE. Why not? Good foreign agents pretending to be

bad foreign agents who are in fact great foreign agents pretending to be Feds. Getting us to help them compromise our own agents.

MYLES. Blaine, if that were true then I can't even believe you are who you say you are.

(**MYLES** *thinks a second. HE quickly points the gun at* **BLAINE**)

MYLES. That's right!

BLAINE. Or why should I believe you are who *you* say you are?

MYLES. Because I know I'm me!

BLAINE. How do I know you're you? What if the who you think you are isn't the who who you really are?

MYLES. Blaine, the trick to siphoning gasoline is not to swallow any.

BLAINE. What if you've been pre-conditioned? Like Pavlov's dog, waiting for some signal to reveal who you really are?

MYLES. Uh… Wait a minute. Then I should give you the gun?

(**MYLES** *tries to hand* **BLAINE** *the gun but he refuses it*)

BLAINE. But what if I'm not who I think I am?

MYLES. Somebody has to take the gun. At least long enough for me to get some aspirin.

(**HALI** *takes the gun and checks the clip*)

HALI. Empty. No weapon and three spies outside.

MYLES. But… but what about all those things of yours I found?

HALI. Myles, everything you ever found was with my help. And I mean everything!

MYLES. Pussycat, please, not in front of Blaine.

BLAINE. I think the idea was for all three of us were to be out of here by now. In your own way you were just trying to keep the two of us alive, right, Hali?

MYLES. Wait a minute. I have to know something first. Who do you love? Me or Blaine?

HALI. I can only answer that in this way. Imagine an agent privy to very special information whose identity was compromised. The spouse of such an agent could be threatened to influence that agent. Unless that agent could prove, say through divorce, their spouse no longer had any meaning for them.

BLAINE. *(with sadness)* ...And if that agent only pretended to like someone else and was merely using them to establish another cover, could they keep the other person out of harms way as well.

HALI. I'm sorry Blaine.

MYLES. You know, I suspected something like that all along. Tough baked beans Blaine. But after all, let's be reasonable.

BLAINE. *(deflated)* I let my heart get in the way of my reason. Well let's see how I can get my head to work now. Let's get to that door before it breaks down.

(**MYLES** *and* **BLAINE** *go to the door and as it bursts open* **MYLES** *and* **BLAINE** *are knocked unconscious to the floor.* **AGENTS LAWSON, MALCOLM** *and* **BRICE** *storm in with guns drawn*)

AGENT MALCOLM. Hold it right there! You're under arrest! Impressive how you managed to yank their strings.

(*With her hands up,* **HALI** *begins slowly backing up towards the control panel*)

HALI. And just what is it I'm supposed to be guilty of?

AGENT MALCOLM. Figure it out for yourself. Just rearrange the letters in "Foreign Agent". You get "One Fine Rat." True, only one is in the criminal code and maybe that's how it ought to be but isn't it telling how both will squeal when cornered.

HALI. You left out two letters.

AGENT MALCOLM. Huh?

HALI. What about the two "g"s? "Foreign Agent" can only

become "One Fine Rat" if you leave out the two "g"s.

AGENT MALCOLM. Ok. I'll give you that. Because I left out only letters. Alone they don't mean anything. But put enough of them together and in the right order and you get the Constitution. The Declaration of Independence. The Vehicle Code of the Department of Motor Vehicles. Maybe I'm a sucker to believe in those things. But until they tell me about it I'll keep my badge and enforce the laws. Because to me justice is more than a word made up of just eight letters.

HALI. Seven letters.

AGENT MALCOLM. Ok. I'll give you that too. Because you're very good at counting Falcon, but you forgot to count one other thing.

HALI. What's that?

AGENT MALCOLM. You forgot to count on us doing our job. And what is this?

(HE picks up the small clear bag containing the catnip)

AGENT MALCOLM. *(Continued)* Jackpot! And I do mean pot! As if being a commie spy weren't bad enough. But Marijuana too! Ok Reefer Red. Let's take a "trip" together. Like to the Leavenworth Federal Penitentiary. Elevation, 1,017 feet. That will be a new kind of "high" for you to experience, courtesy of Uncle Sam. This additional find will make our boss happy.

HALI. Only if your bosses name is whiskers and he likes playing with balls of yarn.

AGENT MALCOLM. His name is J. Edgar Hoover and I don't care what kind of balls he likes to play with. We've done a good job today.

HALI. Too bad your job didn't include spending some time examining the motor housing of this observatory.

*(In a flash, **HALI** presses the button on the control panel and the dome begins moving. SHE breaks the button off and throws it to **AGENT LAWSON**)*

AGENT LAWSON. What are you doing?

HALI. Waiting for two pieces of metal to make contact and close a circuit that will blow this dome sky high when it reaches zero degrees. Got a speech for that one?

AGENT MALCOLM. Yes I do. But it's mostly a lot of four letter words I scream at the top of my lungs.

AGENT LAWSON. Quick! Find the power source. Pull anything!

(As **AGENT LAWSON** keeps HER gun on **HALI**, **AGENTS MALCOLM** and **BRICE** go to a junction box where a series of wires are attached)

AGENT MALCOLM. Maybe it's one of these?

AGENT BRICE. Hurry! 30 degrees and dropping.

(After struggling with one of the wires he yanks it out and dome stops moving)

AGENT LAWSON. Good work, Agent Malcolm.

AGENT MALCOLM. Thank you. You see in my long experience with complicated electronic devices...

(The dome begins to move again)

AGENT BRICE. 25 degrees and dropping!

(**AGENT BRICE** picks up the other end of the disconnected wire)

AGENT BRICE. (Continued) All he did was disconnect the waffle iron!

AGENT LAWSON. Pull another wire!

AGENT MALCOLM. Right.

(**AGENT MALCOLM** struggles with another wire and finally yanks it out. The dome stops moving again. Everyone freezes)

AGENT LAWSON. Oookkkaaayyyy... I... Think... We... Got it.

AGENT MALCOLM. Yes of course. There's always a back up system. I'm not saying I deserve any medals...

(The dome starts moving again)

AGENT BRICE. 20 degrees and dropping!

*(**AGENT BRICE** picks up the other end of the wire)*

AGENT BRICE. *(Continued)* This time he disconnected the coffee machine!

AGENT MALCOLM. An unattended coffee machine is a danger…

AGENT LAWSON. Pull another wire!

*(HE pulls the last wire after a struggle and the dome once again stops moving. Everyone freezes again. **AGENT BRICE** quietly walks over to a table)*

AGENT BRICE. That's funny. The toaster light is out.

AGENT MALCOLM. Oh sure Brice! Make it look like I don't know what I'm doing! See. There are no more wires.

*(**AGENT MALCOLM** hits the side of the wall and a panel opens open revealing several more junction boxes with dozens of wires leading out of them)*

AGENT MALCOLM. *(Continued)* Ah crap.

*(The dome starts rotating again. Myles sees **AGENT LAWSON** holding a gun on **HALI**. HE sneaks up behind **AGENT LAWSON**. and grabs HER taking HER gun away)*

MYLES. No cursing in front of Blaine. He's impressionable you know.

AGENT LAWSON. What are you doing?

MYLES. Saving the day! Run Hali, my love! And bring back the F.B.I.

HALI. Yes my sweet! I won't forget.

*(**HALI** runs out the back door)*

AGENT LAWSON. But we are the F.B.I.

MYLES. More like the F.I.B. I'm guessing.

AGENT LAWSON. Your wife attached a bomb to this place. And if you don't stop this dome rotating we're all of us going to be dead!

AGENT BRICE. 15 degrees and dropping!

MYLES. Oh very dramatic, Agent Brice. But the Valley Theater Awards were last week.

(**AGENT LAWSON** *elbows* **MYLES** *in the stomach and HE doubles over falling to the floor.* **AGENT LAWSON** *grabs HIM by the collar*)

AGENT LAWSON. I'm telling you if you don't stop this dome rotating we're all going to be blown sky high!

(**AGENT MALCOLM**, *knowing what is about to come up, mimics* **AGENT BRICE**)

AGENT BRICE. 10 degrees and dropping!

(**MYLES** *thinks for a second then runs to the electrical panel but then stops short*)

MYLES. Wait a minute… What if you're just trying to fool me. And in fact the observatory blow up only if I interfered with the rotating! How am I supposed to know who is right my friend!

(**AGENT LAWSON** *sighs, places the gun against* **MYLES'** *HEAD and cocks the trigger*)

MYLES. *(Continued)* I guess you're right.

(**MYLES** *goes to a specific part of the floor, does a little tap dance over it and kicks the wall and the dome stops*)

AGENT LAWSON. Quick, Agent Malcolm. After her. If she makes it to the coast a Russian sub is sure to be waiting for her.

MYLES. You mean Hali was a spy after all? The woman I lived with for 3 years? A brilliant resourceful mastermind who couldn't once remember to put the cat out before we went to bed?

AGENT LAWSON. Pull all the recording devices Brice. I'll contact the coast guard. And you… !

(*SHE is face to face with* **MYLES** *backing HIM up towards the wall*)

AGENT LAWSON. *(Continued)* You... ! You... ! You... !

(**MYLES** *kicks* **BLAINE** *who finally gets up*)

MYLES. Wake up Blaine. I think she has something to say to you.

(Barely controlling HERSELF, SHE and **AGENT BRICE** *leave slamming the door as THEY exit. The vibration causes a picture of a galaxy to fall revealing behind it a picture of Khrushchev with a hammer and sickle.* **MYLES** *and* **BLAINE** *eye each other)*

MYLES. *(With a Russian Accent)* So comrade, finally we are free of all the American's recording devices. Dodo, indeed! We made Foolish Federals believe only Hali was agent and not us also. Success!

BLAINE. Too bad Comrade Hali had to leave and not here to celebrate.

MYLES. Necessary sacrifice and her fault. She always traveling in plane with lights on. Stupid for her to get caught in picture, looking like third nipple of constellation Virgo. And always, always she is talking on radio.

(Both **BLAINE** *and* **MYLES** *remove scripts from beneath their clothing)*

BLAINE. *(Also with a Russian Accent)* Yes, believing we have played our parts remarkably well. Addled American Agents never realizing they were mere actors in script we manipulated after we discovering that first microphone by the owl's nest. Hmmm... thinking I maybe should have had a career on Leningrad stage.

MYLES. Your presence go long way in reducing motherlands shortage of ham. Time to going back on spying on American Base.

BLAINE. Yes, and Premier Khrushchev shall be so pleased that the anti-truth serum drug that we have developed has permitted us to lie most effectively to Americans my trusted, wonderful comrade whom I am loving so much.

MYLES. Yes, I can see it is still working.

(**MYLES** *looks out window with binoculars*)

MYLES. *(Continued)* Farwell comrade Hali. Soon she'll be in motherland... Oh moi Bog! Mi imeem problemi! Why is her plane losing altitude? Oh comrade Blaine... sweet little Babushka... While you were siphoning gas out of my car happening to take some from the plane as well?

BLAINE. Well... It does hold hundreds. And I really was low on gas.

MYLES. Did you remember to put the gas cap back on the plane?

(**BLAINE** *thinks a second, pulls a gas cap our of his pocket, looks at it, and places it back in his pocket*)

BLAINE. Yes.

(**MYLES** *puts down the binoculars*)

MYLES. Well whatever happened I can't see her now. Poor comrade Hali. You did remember to put parachute in plane like I asking you?

BLAINE. Yes, I putting in a pair of shoes... parachute... in the plane.

MYLES. Pair of shoes? You said pair of shoes!

(**MYLES** *begins to strangle* **BLAINE**)

BLAINE. Nyet, nyet! Parachute! Parachute! Get a hold of yourself, comrade. You're beginning to hear things.

MYLES. That must be it. I'm still in shock.

(**MYLES** *buries HIS head in his hands and* **BLAINE** *silently mouths the word "oh shit."* **MYLES** *looks up and* **BLAINE** *quickly smiles*)

MYLES. *(Continued)* She'll be caught. She'll talk. And jail for all of us. A perfect plan Kaput! Kaput I tell you, Kaput! Unless of course...

BLAINE. Defect? Nyet, they won't trust us.

MYLES. Not at first but... We'll take that portrait of Eisenhower and reduce it to some nice wallet size pictures for our billfolds. You only carrying around pictures of people you really like. See. I carrying a picture of you.

(**MYLES** *shows* **BLAINE** *a picture in HIS wallet*)

BLAINE. Yeah! And I carrying a picture of...

(**BLAINE** *is about to reach into his pocket to pull out his wallet but stops*)

BLAINE. *(Continued)* That's a good idea!

(The sound of a siren is heard)

MYLES. They're coming back. Might be helping our case is we lose that picture of Khrushchev too.

BLAINE. Right. After all, when you get right down to it the Americans aren't our enemies. The Martians are.

MYLES. Blaine, when agents coming back please let me do all the talking. Martians!

BLAINE. I hope the Americans will let us working for them. I'd hate to spending the rest of my life in a little jail cell. Now I knowing how Toby must have felt.

MYLES. Da. Poor Toby. You know Blaine. I've learned something. If there were such a thing as Martians, I deserving to be captured by them, put in a little cage and subjected to their ridiculous experiments just like he was.

(**MYLES** *and* **BLAINE** *finally remove the portrait of Khrushchev to reveal a hole in the wall with a Martian standing on the other side holding a large net*)

MYLES. Aw crap!

BLACKOUT

End of Play

PROPERTIES

PRESET

50's style radio (on desk)
Box of Band Aids (in desk)
50's style phone (on desk)
Screwdriver, hammer and wrench (by telescope)
Books (on and in desk and filing cabinet)
Papers with graphs (in desk)
Star charts (in filing cabinet)
Magnifying glass (on desk)
Small breakable statue of dog (on desk)
Assortment of personal household items (in filing cabinet)
Box of catnip (in desk)
Hamster glued to side of small cage (on table)
Ham radio set (on desk)
Three microphones (hidden around observatory)
Waffle iron (on desk)
Coffee machine (on filing cabinet)
Toaster (on table)
Portrait of Eisenhower (on wall)
Portrait of Khrushchev (smaller and behind portrait of Eisenhower)

PRESET DREAM SEQUEANCES

Bowls, spoons, knife syrup, butter, glass of orange juice, napkins, muffins, jam (on table)
Black knit cap and sweater (behind cabinet)

PROP TABLE

Three 50's style cameras (one for each agent)
Breakable bird's egg (Blaine)
Ice pack (Blaine)
Box of Filters (Blaine)
Invitation (Hali)
Pictures in wallet (Myles)
Piece of luggage (Hali) containing:
    Three flimsy negligees
    Face powder
    Handcuffs
Binoculars (Mrs. Voskevec)
Small book (Mrs. Voskevec)
Gold coins (Tatianna)
Pack of cigarettes (Myles)
Three guns (one for each agent)
Key for handcuffs (Blaine)
Photograph (Tatianna)

Small walkie talkie (Malcolm)
Thumbscrew (Malcolm)
Map (Lawson)
Note pad and pencil (Malcolm)
Syringe and bottle (Lawson)
Rope and gag (Malcolm)
Earrings (Lawson, Blaine)
Scripts (Myles and Blaine)
Gas cap (Blaine)
Ray Gun and Net (Martian)

COSTUME PLOT

DR. MYLES STANTON: White office shirt with simple dark tie. Tweed pants. A white lab coat.

BLAINE: White office shirt with a garish bow tie. Plain pants. Horn rimmed glasses and with hair slicked down. Five white lab coats as following: 1) In good condition 2) With feathers stuck all over 3) Ripped to shreds as though attacked by wild animal 4) Blackened and burnt and, if possible, with smoke rising from it 5) with green cactus paddles and needles sticking up through out it.

HALI: Bright and colorful summer dress, tastefully sexy. High heels. Later, simple morning dress with apron.

MRS. VOSKOVEC: Serious is not severe gray business suit or dress. Trench coat, fedora and sunglasses. Hair sensibly styled.

RIMSKY: Serious is not severe gray suit, somewhat ill fitting with padded shoulders. Trench coat, fedora and sunglasses. And a Daniel Boone coonskin cap.

TATIANNA: Serious is not severe gray business suit or dress. But tighter, closer to the knee and more loosely buttoned as though in conflict with what she must wear. Hair more attractively styled. Trench coat, fedora and sunglasses. And a Mickey Mouse Club hat with ears.

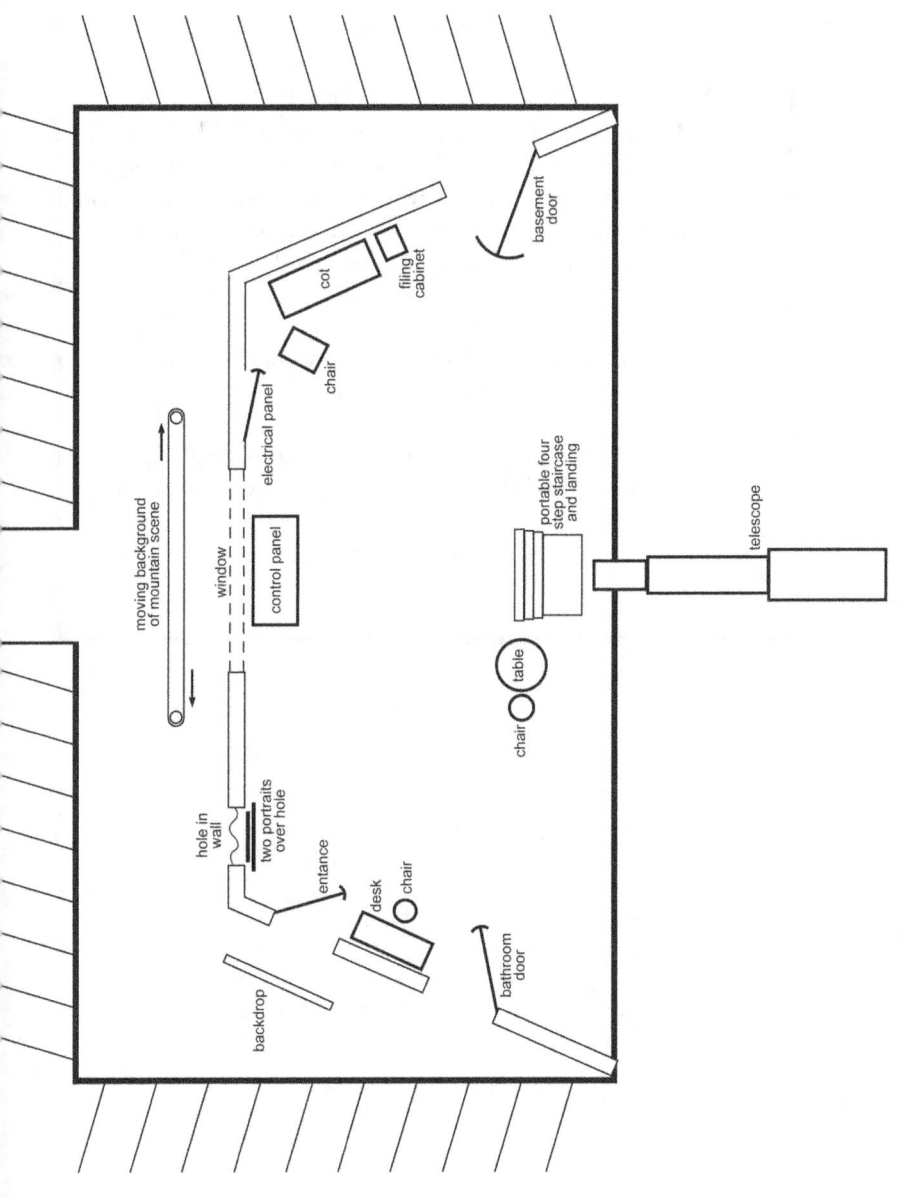

From the Reviews of
KAPUTNIK...

"It's been some fifty years when the "Russies" were thought to excel and lead when it came to the space race. *Kaputnik* shows how these "reds" were just red in the face— the same way that the theater audience will be after having a few good belly laughs!...They may have been first in space, but they still can't write a play as funny as this one!"
– *Accessibly Live*

"Reminiscent of the 1950's, 'Your show of shows'"
– *Back Stage West*

"Falling and sweating and sputtering and strangling his subordinate, Myles is like Homer Simpson, complete with lab coat"
– *L.A. Weekly*

Also by
Frank Semerano...

Murder Me Once

Next Stop, Murder

The Tangled Snarl

Thataway Jack

A Vampire Reflects

Please visit our website **samuelfrench.com** for complete descriptions and licensing information

OTHER TITLES AVAILABLE FROM SAMUEL FRENCH

DEAD CITY
Sheila Callaghan

Full Length / Comic Drama / 3m, 4f / Unit Set

It's June 16, 2004. Samantha Blossom, a chipper woman in her 40s, wakes up one June morning in her Upper East Side apartment to find her life being narrated over the airwaves of public radio. She discovers in the mail an envelope addressed to her husband from his lover, which spins her raw and untethered into an odyssey through the city… a day full of chance encounters, coincidences, a quick love affair, and a fixation on the mysterious Jewel Jupiter. Jewel, the young but damaged poet genius, eventually takes a shine to Samantha and brings her on a midnight tour of the meat-packing district which changes Samantha's life forever—or doesn't. This 90 minute comic drama is a modernized, gender-reversed, relocated, hyper-theatrical riff on the novel Ulysses, occurring exactly 100 years to the day after Joyce's jaunt through Dublin.

"Wonderful… Sheila Callaghan's pleasingly witty and theatrical new drama that is a love letter to New York masquerading as hate mail… [Callaghan] writes with a world-weary tone and has a poet's gift for economical description.
The entire dead city comes alive…"
- *New York Times*

"*Dead City,* Sheila Callaghan's riff on James Joyce's Ulysses is stylish, lyrical, fascinating, occasionally irritating, and eminently worthwhile… the kind of work that is thoroughly invigorating."
- *Backstage*

SAMUELFRENCH.COM

OTHER TITLES AVAILABLE FROM SAMUEL FRENCH

JACK GOES BOATING
Bob Glaudini

Full Length / Comedy / 2m, 2f / Interior

Four flawed but likeable lower-middle-class New Yorkers interact in a touching and warmhearted play about learning how to stay afloat in the deep water of day-to-day living. Laced with cooking classes, swimming lessons and a smorgasbord of illegal drugs, *Jack Goes Boating* is a story of date panic, marital meltdown, betrayal, and the prevailing grace of the human spirit.

"An immensely likable play [that] exudes a wry compassion."
- *The New York Times*

"Endearing romantic comedy about a married couple and the social-misfit friends they fix up. Witty and knowing and all heart."
- *Variety*

"Glides effortlessly from the shallow end of the emotional pool to the deep end."
- *Theatremania.com*

SAMUELFRENCH.COM

www.ingramcontent.com/pod-product-compliance
Lightning Source LLC
Chambersburg PA
CBHW050514020526
44111CB00052B/2334